Teen
SEX,
Adult
RESPONSIBILITY

A Guide for Teen Fathers

Teen Sex, Adult Responsibility
A Guide for Teen Fathers

WritingsbyS@gmail.com

Copyright year: 2021

Copyright notice: by Sylvester H. Edwards Sr.

ISBN 9780578836423

All scripture references are taken from the Holy Bible,
King James Version

This book is dedicated to my mother Robin A. Edwards. A mother who knew how to love and show love through many adverse situations, even in teenage pregnancy.

I Love You Mom.

Teen SEX, Adult RESPONSIBILITY

A Guide for Teen Fathers

Sylvester H. Edwards Sr.

Conversation Titles

Sex

Responsibilities of Sex
Fathering a Child
Teenage Pressure

I'm Pregnant
(What Should I Do as a Teenage Boy?)

Telling My Parents
The Pregnancy and Delivery
Be There

It's Time

Educational Career

Financial Responsibility

Being There

What Not to Do
Your Spiritually Responsible

My Example

Life Goes On

The Outcome
Today's Views of Teen Pregnancy
Giving Back

Facts and Resources for Teen Parents

Introduction

This book is not written as an encouragement to teen sexual activity. Neither is it written to instruct teen boys on how to become a teen father. This book is not written to glorify teenage pregnancy at all. The purpose of this writing is to open the conversation about teenage dads that seem to have been left out of the conversation when discussing teen pregnancy. As one who was a teenage dad and one who experienced the negative and sometimes degrading statements and conversations, actions, and lack of support from others I hope to help the teenage dads of today realize that they are important and that they do have a voice and a say in the life of the child they helped create. As well they have value and bring more to the life of the child than many of the examples that have gone before them.

More than anything I want the world to see teenage dads as more than the bad guy, the one at fault, a no-good person or any of many other negative things usually attached to his name. Teenage dads have feelings and emotions just as teenage moms do. Teen dads go through the same heartaches and decision-making processes as well. It's time we as the adults realize that in order to help curve the teenage pregnancy rate, we have to teach our young people, encourage them, believe in them and if they make a mistake of any proportion, we have to help them overcome with love. Without love none of us would have made it and it takes that same love to help the next generation make it as well.

※

Sex

❧ Sex

As one who is under the age of adulthood the decision to have sex is a big one. Even for those who are adults it is a big decision but for teens even bigger. The reason why is there are very real consequences that can result from the decision to have sex. Not only the most obvious one, which is pregnancy, but also sickness from many diseases. These diseases can attack your body in a variety of ways. Some can cause mental damage and even death if not detected and treated. Another consequence that is often not spoken of enough is the life change that happens when you become pregnant. Not just the life of the female or the child but also the life of the teen dad. Those consequences are compounded for the teenagers who indulge in the act of sex because they often lack the maturity and resources to properly deal with being pregnant.

There are reasons why as a teenager the decision should be to wait until adulthood and after their wedding has taken place. We have heard this all before many times and some plainly disagree. Yet the fact remains, sex after marriage is the best decision any person can make. Some reasons why waiting is best are when two people wait to have sexual relations after their wedding so many things are shared only between them. The time, effort, and enjoyment of learning each other physically that has not been shared with anyone else. This though not taught or enforced as it was in years past, brings about a bond between the two people that truly carries them to a new level of love and commitment. They not only learn to please each other but they learn to trust each other in a way unlike any other. Trust built on sharing this special and sacred physical act strengthens the trust in the bond of marriage and the life they will share together forever.

That leads us to education. It is the responsibilities of the parents of both the young man and the young woman to teach them what sex is, the reasons why sex is important and encourage them to commit to waiting for marriage before having sex. Though many learn in school or from friends it should be taught by the parents who can best answer any questions the teen would have. Those who may not have parental support can learn the truth about sex from a school resource officer, pastor, or trusted mature Christian adult.

What should be taught? First the laws of God through biblical scriptures. It is plain in the Word of God that sex before marriage is against God's desire. 1 Thessalonians 4:3(KJV) Next the education of the repercussions of having sex before marriage. Again, not only is there the possibility of pregnancy but the possibility of disease, sickness, and death. As well the possibility of not knowing what kind of medical issues that can arise as your partner may have had many sex partners and you then become a part of the mix in all that has been done before you. Then there is the life effect of sex before marriage. It can affect you as an individual and even you both as a couple for the rest of your life. So often we say the worst that can happen is that I am locked in for eighteen years. This is not true. You as teen parents can become locked in for the rest of your lives as there is a possibility of birth defects, illness, deformities, mental challenges and more that can affect the growth and development of the child which will cause you to have to care for the child for the duration off their life. If that does become the case, then you will need to properly plan for the care of the child if you become sick or pass away before the child does. This then affects the life of your family members or care givers you chose to carry on the care of the child. A lot to consider which usually does not get the consideration it deserves and so we decide to engage in sex as teens.

Responsibilities of Sex

Who is responsible for the pregnancy? This question is one that mimics the question who is at fault for the fall of man Adam or eve? It is a question that has many angles of view and many considerations of decision. As for the pregnancy and the question who is responsible, it begins with the history of the parents. Was there a history or generational curse that has been passed on to one or both teens? Next is the education of the parents and teens involved or the lack there of. Whether spiritual, home and/or scholastic, sex education is a must and a very important part of the growth development and aid to the decision-making process of teenagers must be considered. Does that say that teens are not capable of making this decision? No, it says that teens are not mature enough.

It says that to make this decision every angle and responsibility of the outcome of the decision should be made known, investigated, researched, talked about, prayed about, talked about again, and prayed about and prayed about once more before the decision is made. Not only will you get the best answer but if you follow the advice given you will make the right decision. That decision will be the decision not to but after this careful consideration process the full understanding of why not will be better understood by both the teenage boy and the teenage girl. If the decision to engage in teenage sex is any other decision it will be both teens that will carry the blame equally.

Fathering a Child

The physical act of sex is the simplest part of becoming a father. It is often misconstrued by teens as the truth of love and intimacy. It is often not properly shared and then not properly understood. When a teenage dad fathers a child is not at the time of conception. Truth is a teenager who fathers a child is a rare occurrence. The reason why it is such a rare occasion is because to father a child is to go through the steps of the chapters to follow and not many teens have the desire, opportunity, time, and resources to do this before their teen years end and the adult years begin. Many become dads and often that is where they stay. This is due to many reasons that could be contributed to the teenage dad as well as the teenage mom and even their family and friends. Yet for those who become fathers it is a path and experience that takes a lifetime, not just eighteen years.

Boys are brought up to be tough and strong. They are taught not to cry and to not to show weakness. They play all types of physically demanding sports like football and basketball as a way of displaying their talents but also as a way of displaying their strength and toughness. They are taught to be a man or some variation of it usually reflective of the experiences of their teacher(s). And what it is to be a man is often colored by the same prejudice experiences of the ones who they learn from. Then there are the experiences each boy has as he grows up in the neighborhood where he lives. These experiences can be some of the most influential parts of his development especially in the teen years. Often drugs are introduced, the opportunity to do the wrong things like get involved with the wrong crowd, stealing, and so much more can influence his mental development.

But then there is the issue of girls. By the time boys get to the beginning of their teen years they instinctually notice the opposite sex and the hormonal changes in their bodies do not help at all. It is a time of crazy change going on while it is also a time of normal development. How boys are instructed and encouraged can make a huge difference in the choices they will make during their teenage years. Remember I spoke of influences and being taught to be a man?

These teachings and encouragement begin to show up in a boy's life about this time. Along with the peer teachings and pressure. The decisions a teen make can easily be clouded so that it is easier to make the wrong decision instead of the correct one.

Teenage Pressure

Being a teen is hard enough on its own but then there is the pressure from teen peers that influence the decisions made quite often. Let's look at playing sports. Will all teenage boys play sports? No, but those who do are more likely to have been encourage by a friend than simply deciding to because they like the game. The same is the case with deciding to participate in a robbery, try smoking and entering the sexually active zone. These and more are also areas of growth and development that peer pressure often affect when a teen is faced with making decisions. For me as a teen, I found this time to be quite challenging. I had been brought up to respect women and told that I should take care of women, but I had also been told to be tough and to be a man. Even as a teen I was encouraged to be a man when making decisions. Those who influenced me the most is the same people who influence most boys. Brothers, uncles, cousins, and even my mom and sisters. The younger males all kind of did what we saw the older guys do and we tried to emulate them as much as we could. It was more than what we saw them do, heard them say but also, I was given access to witnessing things firsthand that influenced me. The same is the case for many teenage boys. They hear older guys talk and are instructed by older guys to be a man while having to make decisions that can affect the rest of their life. The pressure from other teens can way even heavier that the pressure of adults. Teens often compare notes by bragging on the things they have done. Scoring more that someone else in a game, being able to stay out later than another and getting the pretty girls to like them. All of these and so many other things are peer pressure areas of comparison. These same pressure areas carry over into the decision-making process and can cause a teen to make decisions that will change their lives drastically. Like the decision to have sex.

There is also the pressure that comes from the teenage girls. Not all of them intentionally pressure teenage boys but all teenage girls cause pressure on teenage boys. Like girls' boys at the teen stage in life not only notice the opposite sex but begin to have feeling that are new and unexplained. The inability to rationalize these thoughts and feelings while the strength of the pressure to want to know more intensifies can be almost too much to bear. Then a girl walks by who looks good and smells good. That attraction is hard enough to manage but what if she smiles or heaven forbid speaks. That can be the straw that starts the fire in a teenage boy and the heat from the fire then intensifies the pressure every time he sees her. Or any other teenage girl who he finds attractive in any way. As well there is the pressures from adult women. Those who are in his life that are not family and those who are on tv (fantasizing) can be motivating factors for a teenage boy to desire to know more and experience what he has only dreamed of.

With all this happening to the teenagers it is almost easy to understand why the decision to have sex is made. Yet the decision to have sex takes the same energy to make as the decision not to have sex. Again, I go back to the teaching. To the training from the parents as well as the positive encouragement from family and the educational system can weigh heavy on a teen making the right decisions. With all the right teachings and encouragements in place can a teenager still make the wrong decision? The answer is yes. It is very possible for the teens to make the wrong decision despite the training and teaching they receive simply because their emotions, hormones and feelings can be what push them over the line and they decision is made. This can be a very misleading experience as sex is nothing that you have been taught or heard about. It is an experience that is different for each couple as well as for each individual. What is done and how it is done dictates the outcome of the experience for both. So much at stake and so much to chance on the decision to have sex.

I'm Pregnant

What Should I Do as a Teenage Boy?

This is a statement not many teenage dads or adult dads for that matter ever make. I'm pregnant is usually the statement made to us from the teenage girl. Truth is it is the statement we should make to ourselves, our partner and to others who we must share the news with. The reason is because a girl or young lady does not get pregnant on their own unless it was through an intentional fertilization method by a doctor. Most pregnancies are still done the old fashion way, through sexual intercourse. Since it took both of you to create this life you can be assured that both of you will feel the physical, mental, emotional, and social effects of the pregnancy both of you are pregnant. Yes, the young lady or teen girl feels most of the physical and emotional but that does not negate or lesson the fact that both of you are pregnant together and will share the responsibility and experiences of the pregnancy.

So again, the question I'm pregnant, what should I do? As a teen male pregnant with child first realize your responsibility. This does not mean that it is your fault the pregnancy happened. It took the two of you together to create the child and the two of you together carry the responsibility of the pregnancy.

Even though some may say to you that it is your fault, and you should have used protection and some truly believe that the full responsibility belongs to the male but that is not true. Both involved had equal opportunity to discuss and use protections and again they share the responsibility together.

Another thing you should do is take the time to pray and ask God for direction. Can I pray after all of this? Will God listen to my prayer or even help me? The answer to both questions is yes. God knows that you are pregnant. More importantly he knows all that you and the child will ever go through. The act of creating the child was done against his Word and instruction but the life of the child is precious to him.

As well the life of the mother and father are precious to him. Forgiveness for the act is available just ask.

Also know that your prayers for direction will be answered. God will never leave you alone to face the challenges, tests and trials of pregnancy and parenthood. If you need him, you have every right to call on him and to know that he will hear and answer your prayers. If you have not before I encourage you to make prayer a regular part of your life, if for no other reason for your child. Why? The child is not born yet. Even in the womb a child needs prayer. Just like it is recommended that parents talk to and read to the unborn child in the womb it is so much more important that they pray for the child in the womb.

Along with your prayers begin to talk to each other and discuss the lifelong plans you both want to see come to pass in the life of the child. This discussion will probably have many parts and areas to be covered and many of them will need to be discussed regularly as the life of the child goes on. Be open to listen as well as share with each other the hopes, dreams and desires for the child. When you need advice, and it will be almost immediately after you both find that the pregnancy has happened, I recommend you talk to three people. First God. As stated before, he will always be there for you to talk to, call on and to answer your prayers. Secondly Each other. This will be a conversation that will last for at least the first twenty-one years of the child's life. Why do I say twenty-one years? Because at eighteen years of age a child is not fully ready to make all the decisions of life on their own. They will still need guidance and advice from you both on issues like college, relationships, finances, and their own development plus so much more. So, from the beginning establish a line of communication that cannot be broken. It will probably be challenged and may even need to be relaxed at times but never broken. The very life of the child depends on it. Thirdly talk to your parents. This one will be the hardest of all to establish. Most of the time telling your parents that you broke a vase or got into an altercation in school is hard enough. You are nervous, you may stutter, sweat will probably show itself on your forehead but you get up the nerve and you tell them. With this news, all these characteristics will probably be magnified by ten.

How do I tell my parents that I have a child on the way? What do I say to her parents when confronting them? These are hard questions, but they must be answered. You must tell them as soon as possible. What you will find is that you as the male may get the blame initially but after time has passed and emotions begin to settle the truth of equality in sharing the responsibility will come around. Just be honest and forthcoming as soon as possible, it's the best way.

Telling My Parents

For me telling my parents meant telling my mom as she was the single parent in the household. I did not have a relationship with my dad at that time so breaking the news to my mom was my biggest challenge in life up to that point. I asked myself so many times how do I tell her? What will I say? What will she do? Will I live through this? All of these are viable questions and we all as the guy will ask ourselves these and possibly more before we tell our parents, but we must tell them and the sooner the better.

I was sixteen and I decided I had to tell my mom so I ask her if I could talk to her. It was normal for my mom to have an open-door policy when it came to wanting to talk so immediately, she said yes what is it. I went into her room, sat down, and looked at the floor. Not that it would bring me any comfort, but it would keep me from looking at my mom and possibly help keep my nerves intact. I said mom my girlfriend is pregnant. I did not try to cover it up or soften the blow of the news because I was too nervous and wanted to get it over. I was ready for her response to me or at least I thought I was. I had prepared my mind for a tongue lashing and my face for a good slapping, so I braced myself for both. As I gave her the news, she was putting on the final touches of her make up before she would go out to an event. She turned to me and looked me in the eye and with an even toned voice said, "what are you telling me for?" I was dumbfounded and confused. Her next statement has had a lifelong affect and effect on me. She said, "if you make a baby you have to take care that child, I am not going to do it for you." Then she gathered her things and left to go to her event. I sat in that chair in her room for a while wondering what had just happened. I asked myself why didn't she kill me as I expected? She did not yell or slap me. She did not start crying or ask why. All of these where what I expected and prepared myself for. She blew my mind with her response to my news.

I left her room with that statement that she made, and I took it as a challenge. So, I began to make up my mind and my heart that I would take care of my child no matter what without her having to help me in any way. Was that the best thing to do? Yes and no. I needed to step into the place of a father and provide for every need the child would have. I needed to become an emotional, mental, and physical support for my partner as well as for myself. I also needed to be ready to make hard decision if needed to be sure that the child was cared for in every way. What I did though in deciding to do it alone without my mom's help was I cut her off from the child as a grandparent unknowingly. Though I thought I was making the best decision and at the time it was for me, I was also putting up a wall that would block my mom from being a financial, emotional, and mental support to me, my partner, and the child. We must be very careful when making decisions as a teenage dad. Though a lot of them come upon us quickly we must think and pray before we make them to be sure that they are the best decisions overall and for the future.

Your experience will probably be different from mine as we all will experience this in our own way but the foundation of sharing the news and the response from the standpoint of the teenage male will often be very similar. The key is to be prepared by praying before you share the news, understanding the response may be more than you expect, and being understanding that this is a lot to hear from your parent's standpoint and they may need time to fully embrace what you are sharing. Their love for you will not stop but how they engage you will change according to many factors. All in all, they are on your side and they always will be.

The Pregnancy and Delivery

This is where you can come into the picture really strong. Yes, you were a part of creating the life now you can begin to be the responsible male that is there with your partner every step of the way during the birth of the child. In the beginning of the pregnancy your emotional, and mental support will be most important. As she settled into the truth that she is pregnant she wanted a reassurance that you are going to be there with her and for her. She will take your every move as a sign that you are with her and will be there through the pregnancy and beyond.

Be There

So again, here is where you can affect much positivity. Be there as much as possible to talk, share, and encourage. Be there to go to doctor appointments and to decide on where the child will be born. Be there to talk to her parents as needed to help them understand that you are taking responsibility and sharing in the wellbeing of their daughter and the child. This will help them realize that you too are expecting. Nothing will ease tension and give a greater impression than you being there. Now please do not think that I am saying that you need to impress them. That is far from what I mean. I mean that they will be impressed with your involvement and support of your partner and it will also help them realize that you will be there for the child as well. This impresses the parents of both teens but usually the female's parents are really looking for you to be in the position of being there. It is not just what you should do but it is a position you have the full right to hold. Though some parents will want to take over and direct the care of the female, it is your right to take the position of being there and you should.

As the pregnancy progress expect to give more and more of your time energy and resources to support your partner and the unborn child. The need of time will increase as doctor appointments will become more frequent and topics to communicate about will increase. As the teenage dad you will need to be available to satisfy all the requirements needed of you and that means being available to share in every responsibility of the pregnancy. This means your schedule will need to be reprioritized for what is most important to get your time and attention. Not every waking moment will have to be devoted to the pregnancy, but you will have to be available as needed as much as possible. Excuses won't get you out of your responsibility so don't use them. That also includes when you need time to think and plan on your own. Be there for yourself mentally and emotionally by always praying for your own strength and health.

Your resources will need to begin to be reprioritized as well to ensure that the support for yourself, your partner and the child financially will be ready as much as possible. Any other resources that are available to you like a ride to the doctor appointments and more will be needed and should be available as much as possible. Give your resources, usually your parents or a family member, plenty of advanced notice when they will be needed. Communication is the key to managing the needs you will have.

Here is a great way to begin to be prepared. When you first receive the news that you are pregnant begin to save as much as you can for the care of the child. Yes, you are as teenager and yes you may still be in school but that cannot be the excuses you use to not be prepared. You now have to go into a provider mindset and prepare as much as possible. Getting a part time job and helping family members with needed assistance can bring in money to help you prepare. Even starting your own lawncare business for those in your neighborhood can prove to be very financially rewarding. You can do it and you really need to in order to be prepared.

What else can you do? You can suggest walks that will be good exercise and a good time for the two of you to discuss any topics needed for the delivery and the life of the child. You could offer your support over again to reassure her that you are there for her and the child. And you could begin to plan together for the financial responsibilities of child rearing and college. Is it too early to think about these things? Not at all it is the best time. Before the child is born you have the freedom to prepare accounts and finances to ensure that any needs the child has will be covered. There is an old saying that a little goes a long way. That is true and even more so when a little begins before the birth of the child and is continued as the child grows. The two of you or even you on your own can begin saving in state supported accounts or a separate saving just a few dollars a week and over time. That little will amount to much more that you think by the time college rolls around. This is only a suggestion but something I wish

I had done more diligently than I did when my child was on the way.

As the pregnancy enters the last stages the pressures of the child being born will become more real to you both. As the teenage dad you may feel like you don't know what to do. This is where so many teen dads take the easy way out and disappear. This is not the thing to do. To abandon your responsibility to God, the mother of your child, your child, you parents, and her parents is what is done every time a guy leaves a woman pregnant and alone. The best thing you can do is to remember that this is a joyful time for you both. Stressful yes but joyful still. The time is nearing for the birth of your child and the need of that child for you as his/her father is unexplainable. Only you can be the one to fully fulfill that need and the importance and affect it can have on the life of the child is immeasurable.

As the time get closer the doctor appointments will become much more frequent and the support needed for her will increase dramatically. All the planning that the two of you have done is now about to go into effect and there is something you can do to help ease the pressures of it all, pray. Ask God to help you to be there no matter what. Ask for mental and emotional strength for yourself and your partner. Ask for complete health for the mother and the baby being born. Ask for a good relationship between the families. Ask for continued direction and guidance in the raising of the child. Ask for caring and helpful teachers throughout the child's educational career. Ask for blessings that will help eliminate financial and resource needs for the life of the child. Ask that God will make friends for the child that will be lifelong friends. Friends who will pray with the child and pray for the child. Friends that can be relied on and that will be true friends in every way. Ask for direction in your own life and guidance as you grow as a young man and father. Ask for the same guidance and direction for the mother of the child. Ask for educational blessings and resources that will help you both complete and reach the educational goals that you have. Ask for all that your heart can and continue asking as you continue a prayer life throughout your life and the life of the child.

It's Time

It's Time

The day comes when you get the call that the bay is coming. You could be at school, or at work. You could be on the basketball court or at home studying. You could be with your partner and the call is her vocal cry, it's time. Your response will need to be immediate but not rushed. Let me explain. If you are not in the presence of your partner when the call comes there are some answers you should be given and if not ask the questions to get them. Where is your partner? How is she doing? How close are the contractions? Did her water break? What-estimated time will she be arriving at the hospital? Who will be a person of contact to keep you informed until you get there? Is there anything you need to bring to support her during the pregnancy? While obtaining this information you can judge how immediate you need to get to the hospital to be at the side of your partner. Now yes, you will want to move as quickly as possible, but you must be aware of and obey all traffic laws, as well as the family laws. Who needs to be informed in your family and how much time you have to inform them? Who needs to go with you to the hospital as I recommend that you take someone with you? Let them drive while you are getting the information you need to be there as quickly as you can and to be prepared when you arrive. Sounds like a lot and it is, and it will need to be done most often in a very short amount of time. Some of it can be done in advance and that will help tremendously but the rest will be on the minute tasks once the arrival time comes so please prepare and even practice in advance.

The time has come for the baby arrive. Now you and your partner will have the opportunity to share this life changing experience with others. Only a few will be allowed in the delivery room so if you can decide in advance it will help make things go smoothly. If it is an on-the-spot decision be mindful of her needs as she will probably ask that her mom be there with her. You, the doctor, and staff are the only others who usually are allowed. Some hospitals will allow two supportive people the opportunity to be in the room during the delivery. Along with her mom usually the offer is extended to your mom as she has experienced childbirth and can be a great support for you both. If not available, then a sister or other close female relative can share in the experience if you both desire.

The doctor is in position and gives the instruction to push. Do not think it odd if you push along with her. It is a natural reaction to what is the most important moment in the life of a child and the parents and as a teenage father you may simply not know anything else to do. Remember to encourage your partner during this process because remember you both are responsible. She will need and appreciate your encouragement. If not right at that moment, definitely once the baby is born. Why not right at that moment? Some ladies when put under the pressure of childbirth lash out at the father of the child out of the pain and stress of delivering the child. Some use medicines like pain managers and epidurals to help relax them, ease the pain, and help with the stress of childbirth. What you can do is simply be ready for a temporary change in her demeanor in case it happens during this momentous occasion. As well be ready for a change in her physical body. Childbirth presents a different view and an eye-opening view as well of how a female's body produces a child. You will be surprised to see his change happen and you will gain a new respect for the female body as well.

Once the baby is born you will usually be offered the opportunity to cut the umbilical cord. This signifies that the childbirth has been completed and it is an experience that cannot be explained only experienced. Teenage young men do not often get that opportunity and some run from it. I recommend you take the opportunity to do so. Just as you have been responsible through the pregnancy and now the delivery, enjoy the responsibility of the final step of childbirth. Once the child is born you will immediately feel the weight of being a father and it will change the way you see everything in life. Embrace the change and flow with it. You are now a teenage father and you can do this. Don't be discouraged or feel like the demand is too great. It is the same demand every man and teenage father feels when a child is born especially the first child. Remember the foundational prayers that you prayed and trust God to carry you through. He will, trust me he will. He did it for me and I am a witness that he will do it for you.

Educational Career

Here is where you can begin to make a true difference in the life of your child. Get your education and do not stop until you reach your goals. The importance of your education becomes greater now that you are a teenage dad. You must be able to compete in the marketplace for financial resources, positions in the job market, and the ability to provide for your child. Though they all connect to each other each is and has its own importance for you and your child. Financial gain is the ability to grow in your financial holdings. In other words, the ability to make money. Education is the key to learning and maximizing your ability to make money. You could work a job and just get by but why just get by when you can get ahead. Use the resources available to help you and your partner complete your educational goals. It will mean a better life for you both and the child you are now raising.

You will also see a huge benefit as you compete in the job market due to you finishing your educational career. Employers look at what you bring to the table and your education is your foundation of what you can offer. Those who go to college have a greater opportunity to obtain the positions offered than those who did not but know how to do something. Finishing college is a must for you both, do not let the pressures and challenges in life stop you from reaching that goal. Even if it takes a little longer that you desire do not stop until you reach it, and do not quit. You will be in a much better position to provide of the needs that you child will have and much easier with the education you gain. Your salary depends on it and so does your lifestyle. Make goals and make a commitment to yourself and your child that you will live and provide a good life in a safe environment then make it happen. Education is the foundation stand on it and soar to the top.

❧

Financial
Responsibility

This is where I want to explain to you that you not only have a financial responsibility, but you can meet it even as a teenager. When I became pregnant at seventeen, I decided that I would be a provider for my child always. I began working part time after school as a janitor. It did not really pay enough to cover all the financial needs, but I was not the only one responsible to provide. I was responsible to provide as a teenage dad and so I did. I remember working and getting my first paycheck. I walked to the store five blocks away to buy my daughter's first box of pampers. I was proud to be her dad and proud to be able to provide. It was a rewarding feeling to use my money to get her what she needed. As well it was a rewarding comfort for her mom that I would be there and that I would provide. Yes, we were both teenagers and both in school. Did we have all that we needed? Yes, but that was with the help of her parents and mine. But to be able to go and get what my daughter needed was monumental for me as a teenage dad.

As time would go on, I would work until the job ended and then try to gain other jobs during the summer to help supplement the financial needs for the child. There were times when working was harder to manage because of my schoolwork and then sometimes jobs ended. So, before I graduated high school, I struggled but somehow kept up an ability to provide.

We did not do it alone. We use the resources available to us as teen parents and those resources were absolutely needed. Resources from church's, state programs, local or city programs and more were available and very useful. It is not shameful to need help, but it is a shame if help is available and you do not take advantage of it to provide for you child. Being a man does not mean not needing help it means knowing and accepting help when needed and available. I did not want to get help because I was a very proud teenager, but I realized the need of my daughter outweighed my level of pride. As a teenage dad you may experience a similar challenge. I hope you do not, and I hope you have all that you need to provide everything you child needs but if you find that you need help get help. It is available in so many ways and from many different resources.

Being There

Being There

To be there for many is automatic but for so many it is nonexistent. Being there is usually broken down into three different categories. First and foremost be there for yourself. You as a teenage dad will have to be there mentally emotionally, physically, financially, and educationally for your child and your partner but who is there for you? Often the answer is no one.

When I was told that I would be a teen dad I found my mom's words encouraging in its own way, my sibling's words of support were helpful, and the words of her family were mostly positive but who was there for me? I had to learn to be there for myself. That meant encouraging myself that I could be successful as a dad at the age of sixteen. That meant preparing myself for the mental and emotional roads that had already begun to affect me. That meant preparing myself physically to become a worker in the workforce to provide for my child all that I could while continuing to finish my high school career. It meant being ready for the backlash that could come from her family (thankfully there wasn't much). It meant growing up overnight into a role of a father. Always know God is there for you. He is a resource that will never run out or be too busy to help. Be sure to communicate with him as often as needed and he will be there for you.

What Not to Do

The importance of what a teen dad should not do carries the same weight as what he should do. It also weighs very heavy on the life of the child and must be made clear to the teenage parents. First a teenage mother must realize, as stated before, that this is a different and difficult time as she is now experiencing changes and challenges in every part of your being but so is the teen dad. It is not uncommon for a teen mother or an adult mother for that matter to experience emotional changes due to the imbalance of hormones during and after pregnancy. What you have to be aware of through it all is that there is someone else who are experiencing some challenges as well and the best way to deal with the challenges you both are experiencing is to communicate. This does not mean making accusations or giving blame to the other party. It does not mean taking the side of those around you to be against the teen dad. It also does not mean that you have a license to degrade, talk down to, cut off from the joys of pregnancy or demand things that may not be able to be provided right away. In other words, be considerate of your partner the same as you want him to be mindful of you.

For the teen dad you have to become what you may not have had yourself. What you cannot do is continue a cycle of abandonment or neglect that may have been your experience with your father. Many young boys grow up without their father and some without a father figure all together. When they become parents, it can show in the decisions they make and the lack of interest or commitment to the child or the teen mom. It is almost an automatic reaction to leave or not take on the responsibilities of being a teen dad because your dad didn't do that for you. This is not what you should do. Just as your life was left missing an important relational experience so will the life of your child if you do what was done to you. Children do not ask to come into the world so we as dads must remember that and take on the role as a father fully and without looking back. It is going to be a challenge and the easy thing is always to run. The truth is the best thing overall for the child is for you to stay. Stay and be the change in your child that only you can make, a positive change. As well staying and breaking the cycle will bring positive change in the legacy of your family.

Next do not let the responsibility of a new life cause you to make the wrong decisions. As teens we all are faced with or see others who make the wrong choices. Some choose drugs, others choose alcohol, and some choose crime. All of these are wrong decisions and decisions you want to avoid making. All of these ultimately can cause you to end up in the same place, prison. The choice to indulge or the choice to violate someone else usually is made under the pressures of life. Those who do not have what they need or those who want what they cannot afford choose to indulge in bad decisions as a way of life. All these eventually will cause you to lose time and possibly your opportunity to be an effective dad.

Of all the things that you can do over again making a first impression and redeeming or getting back lost time are two of many things that we can never get to do again.

Don't miss what is right there in front of you, your opportunity to change a life, change the cycle in your family and possibly change the world through your commitment to your child. God is trusting you. Your partner is counting on you and the child is depending on you. Do not leave your child without a father. Do not disappoint God, the child, the teen mom, your family, and hers, and do not disappoint yourself.

Your Spiritually Responsible

As a teen parent you are responsible to share in providing the spiritual foundation for your child. Though some may not have had a spiritual foundation or a proper one the responsibility falls on you to be sure that your child knows the truth of many of the age-old questions. Questions like where is God? Where does God live? Why can't I see him? Is God a man or woman? Where is heaven and so many others. These are all question most of us had as kids. One of the most important life provisions happened when we were given the basics of faith and belief in God. Proverbs 22:6 teaches that we are responsible in the training of our children. Their life outcome depends on it.

If you did not have a spiritual foundation you may be thinking that you can't teach that. My response to you is "yes you can". Take the time to talk to the pastor of a Bible believing church that believes in Jesus Christ. Here you should find the help you need to build your own spiritual foundation and the tools needed to help you do the same for your child. Remember it does not have to be done overnight but the earlier you start the better. Not only will it help you help your child it will also help you help yourself. Trusting in God is the key to making positive changes and choices in your life.

My Example

I was blessed to have a grandfather who I was very close to. We were like best friends and I could confide in him at any time. He advised me and supported me and never gave me a negative word. He helped me see myself as a successful dad by pointing me into the right direction and being an example of what it was to work and provide, while guiding me without a compass into the right direction for the sake of the child. He helped me be there for myself by being there with me.

Most teenage dads do not have that same support but do have a brother or friend male role model that they can trust to listen and advise them in their new responsibilities. If you did not have a support or feel as if you cannot get that support, reach out to a pastor, counselor, school official or the pregnancy hotline for help. Yes, the pregnancy hotline can direct you as the dad to resources that can help you as they do for the mothers. Don't walk through this alone. Proverbs 11:14 (KJV) reminds us that safety is in the multitude of counsel. That safety can be the difference of you being the best dad ever or being a dad that struggles mentally and emotionally even before the child is born.

Secondly be there for you partner. As you have now realized your new responsibilities realize that she has the same responsibilities and more. She will have to care for the child in every way that you will but also will be the one who carries the child, deals with the hormonal changes, attitude swinging, feet swelling, back aches, body changes, and the delivery. With that said she will need your support in every way. She needs to know that you are there emotionally to help keep her mind strong. She needs to know that you are there physically, and she is not in this alone. She needs to know that you will be there to help her through the changes in her body and there to support her in the delivery of the child. Sounds like a lot and it is but it is a part of the responsibilities that you are required to carry.

You should also be there for her spiritually through prayer. Pray for her as much as you can and if she does not have a spiritual foundation help her build one. Again, do not run off and leave her alone to go through all these things by herself. Remember it took both of you to create this child and it will take both of you and more to provide everything this child will need in life. Be ready, be responsible, be there.

Lastly, be there for the child. Now this is last but certainly not least. The child will need at least twenty-one years of love, support, financial, emotional, physical, educational, medical, and social support as well as a commitment of your time. Time to teach as well as time to learn from the child. Time to play and time to discipline. Time to share alone and time to share together with others. Time for sports and time for other interests. Most importantly, time to pray for the child and time to teach the child to pray. The importance of a spiritual life is greater than any other category of life that we experience. Again, pray for their health, pray for their future. Pray for their friends that

God will give them Godly friends. Pray that they will be a Godly friend to others, pray for their mind and the educational career they will have to embark upon. Pray for their life and the children they will one day bring into the world. Pray. There are so many things that you can pray for and with your child that will give them the example and the education on how to pray. Before you teach them to sing a song, or dance a dance, or write their name or remember their address be there for them, teach them to pray. It will be the one thing they will need most of all during their lifetime.

Life Goes On

So many times, when we have children at an earlier age than recommended (as a teen) or even at a more expected age (young adulthood) we feel like it's all over for us. We are now doomed to be parents and give all that we are to our child and that is true. Yet it is also true that if you stop living you will surely die. What we must remember is that thought as a teen you now are a parent and carry all the responsibilities of the position, life goes on for you too. A part of the reason you should continue the education endeavors and obtain all that you can is so that you can build a life of provision love and happiness for your child but also for yourself. If you take all you have and give it away, you have nothing. Your child would not want you to go lacking so that they can be spoiled and that also applies to your life. Live your life every day in the beauty of God's Holiness that he has given you. Yes, be a parent and the best that you can but be an individual who enjoys the journey of life as you live it.

Just like I suggested that you should finish college also finish obtaining the desires you have in life for yourself. Open your own business, take a vacation, write a play, star in a movie, publish a book, spend time with the elderly, build a house and don't stop moving forward. These are just some of the things we desire to do and having a child as a teen can make us believe that these things are now out of reach. That simply is not true. Though you have a child you also must live. The cliché is "all work and no play make Jack a dull boy." Remember your life is just that, your life and you should live it to the fullest while enjoying it to the max. Another saying is "you only come this way once" and its true so while you are here enjoy the happiness God has given you while you create a happiness for the child, he has entrusted to you.

What I Realize

So many times, and at many stages in the journey I have sat down and meditated on the life I have lived and the choices I have made. For me growing up was a challenge and not always a financially easy one. Having parents who loved me through their own life challenges and decisions helped me a great deal yet also created challenges for me. The thing is I had to realize that my life and the choices I make will be my responsibility and some day may create challenges or opportunities for the child that I had created. I would sit in my room and dream of what kind of dad I would be. At the same time, I was asking God to help me be better to my kid than my parents were to me. I believed that it would make the process and journey of being a parent an easier one. Did it? I really do not know but I can say that prayer didn't hurt.

The Outcome

As I began to embrace the responsibilities of parenthood, I realized that I would have to prioritize everything in my life and periodically re-prioritize them to accommodate the changes and needs of life. I began to look at what I had, which was not much tangibly but a great deal of love and support that surrounded myself and my partner. I realized that the choice to become a dad was a premature choice including the acts that it took to get me there, but I could overcome the bad decisions by making better decision going forward. I would need to pray continuously, focus on my life and the life of the child, make solid decisions, and commit to myself, God, and the child to never stop doing my absolute best to be the best dad that I could. I realized that I could make it and I worked daily to fulfill that realization. I worked hard to complete my high school career.

While in high school I decided to join the Army Reserves as an assurance that benefits, and finances would be in place for me and the child. As stated before, I began to work part time jobs even before the child was born to prepare for the financial responsibilities we together as parents would be facing. I also began to make concessions to support my partner in her endeavors of life as she too would need to work hard to complete the high school career and further her education or begin an employment career so that we could solidify a successful future for our child and ourselves.

I must say that as time went on and things would happen, we did not continue in the relationship that we had but we did continue to parent together. We would have a total of three kids together all girls and we worked to provide them with all of life's necessities and many of the wants that they desired. We agreed that we would share in the financial responsibilities without following the path of court and child support that so many before us had resulted to. We agreed to be adults when it came to the life and needs of our children no matter what. Were there tough times and challenging moments along the way? Oh yes there were but together we held on to the commitment we made to parent together and always provide what was best for the children over all else.

After going our separate ways, we both embraced new relationships and worked to build our lives. Today I am happily married with three other children, all boys. Two from this union. As well the girl's mom has given birth to another daughter and is happy in the life she leads and now together from our own lives we offer the love, support, advice when needed and encouragement that we always have for or children and grandchildren, yes grandchildren.

Today our girls have grown into beautiful young women all following the career path they desire. Marriage has happened for our oldest daughter and we are grandparents through that union as well as grandparents even more. Not only are all three of the girl's successful women but they are successful in the lives they live outside of their professions I believe because of prayer and our parental commitment to them. Again, were there changes and challenges as they grew? Yes, but like with any other parent we did our best to guide them from the crib to the stage of graduation from college and beyond.

Just like it worked out for me and my family it can and will work out for you. I always say if you want to achieve what I have achieved, do what I have done. Pray, commit, love, provide, resolve, embrace, challenge, and accept. These will all come into play in your life as a teen dad continually but never give up. You can make it and I am sure that you will. Keep God first, second and third and everything after that must fall in line in your favor.

Today's Views of Teen Pregnancy

Today teen pregnancy continues, and teens continue to struggle with the outcome of the decisions they have made. There are television shows that display many lives involved in the epidemic. I call it an epidemic because for more years than can be counted teens have been dealing with the challenges of pregnancy. For many years it was kept silent as much as possible and when it became a talked about thing it was to talk about the shame and blame and made into a social issue. This happened so locals could get governmental resources, some religious reasons, some social and educational reasons but they all were financial reasons.

Today teen pregnancy is not publicized quite as in the recent past as much as the statistics show a reduction in the percentages. Yet for those who do experience the challenges, highs, lows, disappointments, fears, emotions, mental pressures, physical changes, and life altering thing we know as teen pregnancy it has gone nowhere at all. As for the television shows some are well done with a desire to show the evidence and truth of teen pregnancy to the youth of today. The more we see the evidence on television the more we hope it will help the next generation. Just as importantly billboards and hotlines are displayed where teen moms can call in for help. What I have noticed is that the teen dads still do not get the same consideration and supports as the teen moms. Some are mentioned and given a chance to be heard, but overall, the dads are left to figure things out on their own. Thanks to family members and church leaders, men's groups, and online resources teen dads can find help, support, and encouragement. Some resources for teen dads are listed below. Please use them as needed to help you be the teen dad you desire to be.

Giving Back

For those teens who have been thrust into parenthood you have found out the truths about what it takes to raise a child. You now know that your parents have gone through a great deal to protect and provide for you over the years of your life. Now you have the responsibility to protect and provide for the life you have created.

For both the teen Dad and the teen Mom the desire should be to at the very least give your child the same things you were afforded as you grew up.

Hopefully, your desire will reach far beyond that and you will work to protect and provide for your child in ways that your parents may not have been able to do and with resources that were not available to them. Your desire should be to grow your child into adulthood through love, laughter, educational excellence, determination and again love.

You should also want to give back to the generation you are a part of and the generations to come after you by sharing your experience of teen parenthood. Giving back does not mean giving financially only. If you are in the position to do so those contributions will be welcome by resource centers in n your area and all over the country. But you can be a help by encouraging others through the experiences you have had. From the decisions you made that thrusted you into parenthood to the challenges, ups and downs and more that you experienced because of teen parenthood.

You should look at the future and do all that you can to help stop teen pregnancy. That may mean talking to and praying for your peers and those around you. It could mean sharing in community events as well as publishing a written work to help others not experience what you have experience too soon. You should want to use all your creative ability to spread the word that teen pregnancy needs to stop. Remember, I know how hard it is to be a teen parent and how hard it can be when you are not supported much at all. You can do for others what I hope this book has done for you and that it to encourage you and educate you in the process. Not how to become a teenage dad but the opposite how and why not to. As well I hope you will use the resources mentioned and any other resources that are available to you while sharing the information with others who may be in the same place that you are.

As you read, I am sure that by now you realized there were a few things that repeated quite a bit. Those repeating themes were the things that have the most influence on who you are now and who you will become. Being there Sex and the responsibilities of it, the Pressures teens endure and Teenage fatherhood. Being There before and after the delivery and the Financial duties of fatherhood. Education and the education of the teen mother as well as Life Goes On are all things that every teen parent must deal with. For the teen dad it is immensely important all these themes and any others that may pertain to your situation are given the utmost attention and seriousness to help you reach every level of success that you desire to reach as a teen dad and even as an adult dad.

Remember you can be a positive and successful teen dad. I believe in you and I know you will reach the level of success as a dad that you desire to be. No matter what happens keep God in every aspect of your life. Through hard times and challenging times God will be there to help you be all you desire to be.

My prayer is that God will help you as he did for me. I pray that you realize the importance of being there. I pray that you realize the need of the child and the future you are responsible to provide. I pray that you work together as parents and commit to the child to always parent together no matter what life brings. I pray your success in your life endeavors and success in the mother of your child's life endeavors also. I pray that God will do for your child what he has done for mine and so much more. I pray for your instinct and ability to discern every evil work in the child's life. I pray your strength and stamina as a young man. I pray that both families will work together to support and help bring happiness only into the life of your child. I pray that you live and enjoy life while being all that your child needs you to be in their life. I pray that you always maintain a prayer life and that God grant you blessings beyond your imagination. I pray that you break every evil stigma and generational curse that has followed your family bloodline. I pray for abundance in every area of your life and the life of the child. I pray that your child grow in the love and fear of God and that God will get all the glory out of your life and the life of your child. I pray the love of God be ever present in your life as you raise your child and all the days of your life. It's my prayer for you and every child that will be born through the legacy of your family and that God will cover and protect, provide, and empower you all forever in Jesus name, amen.

❦

Facts & Resources for Teen Parents

Facts

After increasing by 9 per cent in the period 1976-80 in the United States, pregnancy rates declined by 4 per cent between 1980 and 1984 (from 111.9 to 107.3 pregnancies per 1,000 women aged 15-44 years). Between 1984 and 1985, the rate rose by less than 1 per cent to 108.2.
https://ajph.aphapublications.org/doi/abs/10.2105/AJPH.78.5.506

The pregnancy rate in 1984 was 231 per 1000 sexually active women. This means that in 1984, 23 percent of sexually active teenagers would have become pregnant.

In 2018, the birth rate among 15- to 19-year-old girls and women was less than half of what it had been in 2008 (41.5 births per 1,000).
Ncbi.nlm.nih.gov

Resources

❖ What to Expect, www.whattoexpect.com

❖ Parents, www.parents.com

❖ Primer Magazine, www.primermagazine.com

❖ Raising Children Network, www.raisingchildren.net.au

❖ Local Health Departments

❖ Church or Religious Leader

Appreciations

This is where I want to say thank you to those who helped me reach this point in life and in my effort to share with the world. First, I thank God for being my everything, I want to thank again my mom the late Minister Robin Edwards for being the best mom ever, I love you always and forever. I also want to thank my second mom Chief Apostle Olive C, Brown. I cannot count or name all the lessons I have learned from you. I also cannot thank you enough for you hearing and saying yes to God when I was around seven years old. I love you so much. I want to thank my wife Natalie Edwards for being my best friend and my strongest support. I love you Babe. Thank you to my kids three of which I began parenting at sixteen. You girls are an inspiration to me, my sons all are awesome and super supportive to me as well. I also thank my family and friends for your support all my life.

There are some special people who have supported me professionally and I want to name them here. Dr. John Kinney (The Dean, Uncle John), Dr. Ray McKinzie (Uncle Ray), Dr. Lakisha Lockhart (Bestie), Dr. Patricia Gould-Champ, Sharvette Michell (Mitchell Productions), Ifedayo Greenway (She Unveils), Jovan Adams (Manifold, LLC).

www.ingramcontent.com/pod-product-compliance
Lightning Source LLC
LaVergne TN
LVHW021546080426
835509LV00019B/2870